T0193390

Lots of Limericks
Quintillas Cómicas

Silly Poems
in
English
Spanish
Spanglish

written and illustrated by
Mama Bear Gina

Lots of Limericks Quintillas Cómicas
Silly Poems in English Spanish "Spanglish"

iUniverse books may be ordered through booksellers or by contacting:

iUniverse
1663 Liberty Drive
Bloomington, IN 47403
www.iuniverse.com
1-800-Authors (1-800-288-4677)

Library of Congress Control Number: 2019907479

ISBN: 978-1-5320-7702-9 (sc)
ISBN: 978-1-5320-7703-6 (e)

Print information available on the last page.

iUniverse rev. date: 06/18/2019

Para Mi amiga Clara

for my friend Clara

Limericks are such fun!
They can be read by most anyone.
But my books didn't sell,
(at least not very well).
As a Millionaire, I'm all done!

La Gran Quintilla Cómica...
La risa da estrés gastronómica.
Pero el montón en la tienda....
Parece que no se recomienda.
¡Lástima que no gané fama económica!

Me contaron de un Gran Oso.
De leyenda, era super poderoso.
Una abeja le picó.
En seguida lloró.
¡En fín, no era tan peligroso!

Sausage, hash browns, scrambled eggs,
Pancakes, bacon, and frog legs?
It's "All You Can Eat."
My eyes say, "Oh, Sweet!"
But my stomach aches. "STOP!" it begs.

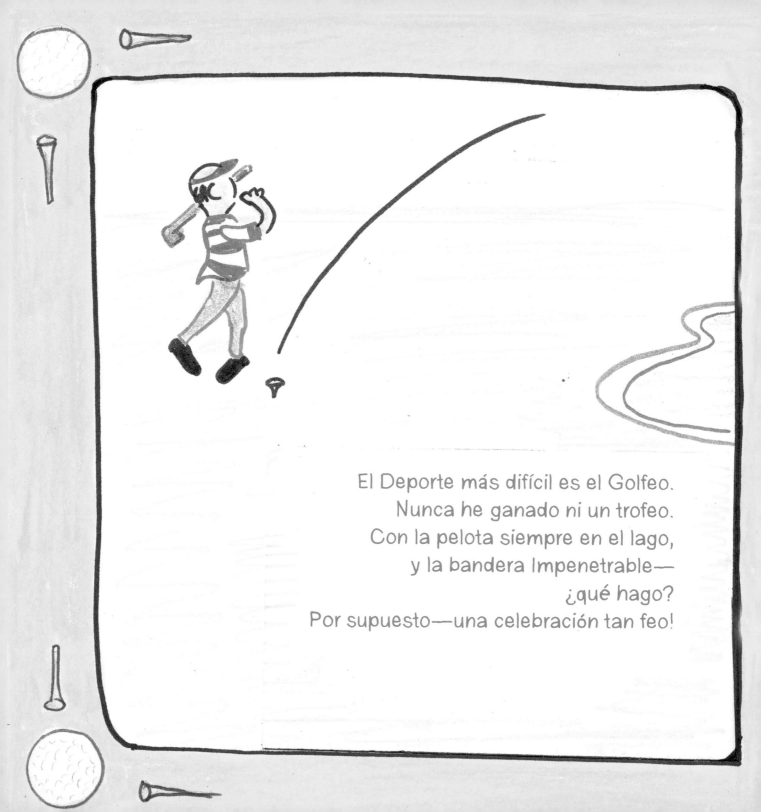

El Deporte más difícil es el Golfeo.
Nunca he ganado ni un trofeo.
Con la pelota siempre en el lago,
y la bandera Impenetrable—
¿qué hago?
Por supuesto—una celebración tan feo!

Yum! Cheesy, Sooey pupusas! ¡Deliciosas!

Today, I ate a pupusa.
Se calló onto my blusa.

I cried for a while,
then threw it on the pile.
¡Toda mi ropa está sucia!

We're in the marching band…
the best one in the land!
The trumpets are fine,
the drums all in line.
And the majorette—
give her a hand!

Me gustan comer albondigas
All covered in spicy tomato sauce
I'm always ready
for a plate of spaghetti
y pan de ajo. ¡No me digas!

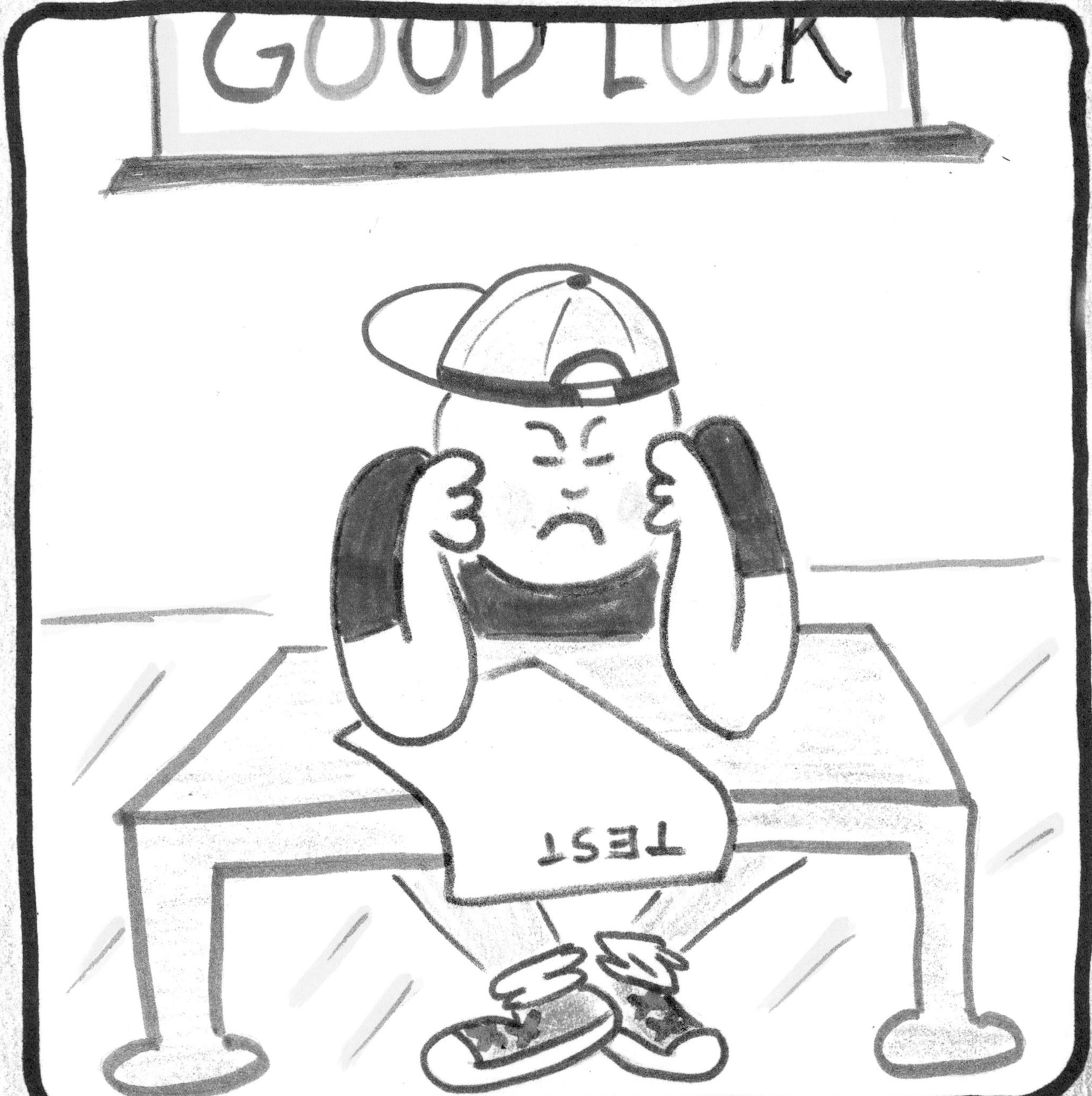
GOOD LUCK
TEST

Ni Lápiz, ni pluma, ni lapicero.
It's only the first day of enero.
My resolution this year:
"Be prepared." But I fear
without them, I'll get a big Zero!

My abuela's name is Gina.
She likes to cook en la cocina.
She once spilled the beans
all over her jeans.
Oops! ¡Frijoles y vaselina!

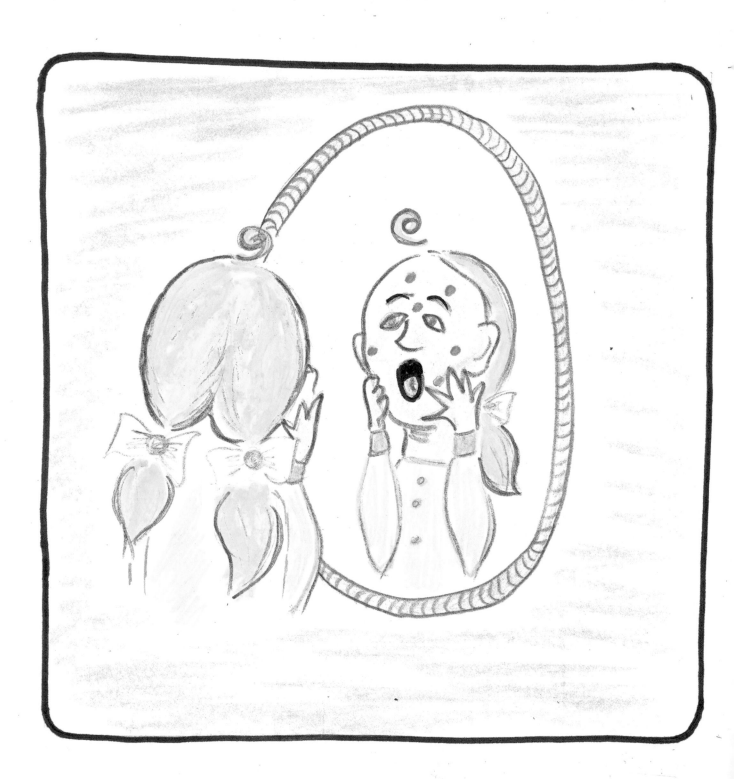

Uno, Dos, y Tres.
I'm looking at my face!
A pimple aquí,
A freckle allí,
Prefiero que no hay ni un trace.

De Costa Rica es ese "Tico."
Es el hombre lo más simpático.
Si le preguntas por qué
sonríe every day,
¡Es porque come mucho Gallo
Pinto!

Tambor, guitarra, o violín.
The piccolo—¡qué chiquitín!
There's no time to lose.
Which one should I choose?
Of course! El Gran Flautín!

The twins named Jack and Jake
took a swim in "Forbidden Lake."
But when they got out
you could hear them shout

'cause their clothes...
"somebody" did take.

Ms. Little speaks golden words
that fly and swoop like birds.
But when her students are bad
she gets REALLY MAD.
and her goldenness sounds really slurred.

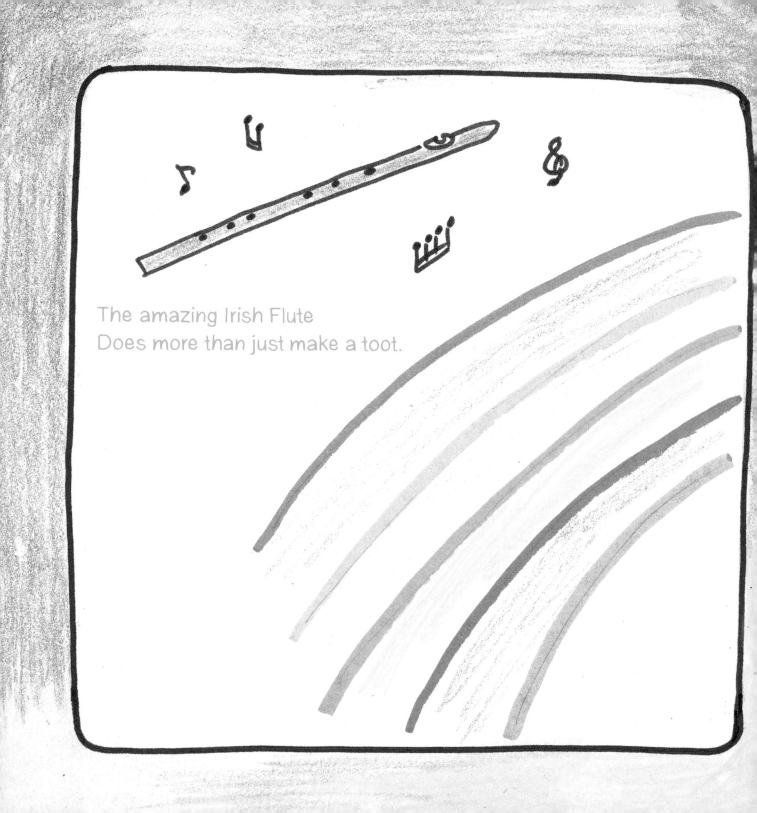

The amazing Irish Flute
Does more than just make a toot.

Pero la gente llorando
y los perros ladrando,
Pues, nadie me quiere escuchar.

Papas fritas, hamburguesa.
All for me on esta mesa.
Un montón de helado,
chocolate cake y gelato.

Too much!
¡Tengo un dolor de cabeza!

Mr. Pickles is a hot mess
He tried, but he had to confess:
"I spilled all the paint.
An artist, I ain't.
But a sculptor, more or less."

Se me chocó el brand new car.
It was my favorite by far.
A mí, no me culparon.
Autografías se firmaron
Because I'm a movie star!

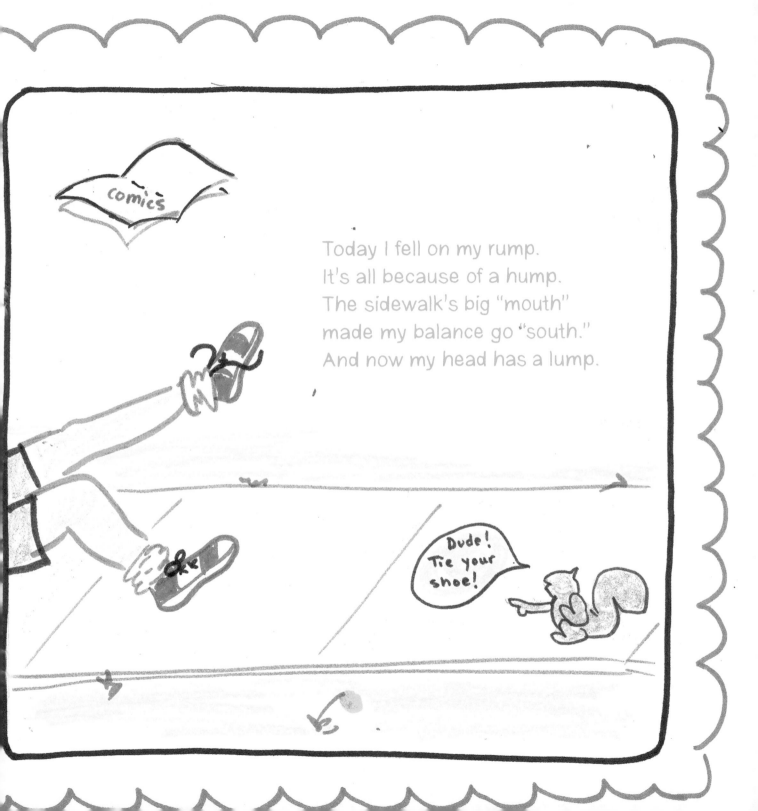

No hay más cosas to upend.
Los carácteres son "on the mend."
I could write forever
about people, or whatever.
Pero en realidad, this is THE END!

GLOSSARY (English – Spanish)

Amazing – Glorioso
Beans – Frijoles
Brand new – Nuevo
By far – Entre todos
Choose – Escoger
Clothes – Ropa
Dress – Vestido
Forbidden – No Permitido
"Give her a hand" – un aplauso. por favor
'God Bless You" – ¡Salud!
Golden – Como oro
Hump – Parte elevado
Jeans – Pantalones
Kalamazoo – Una ciudad en el estado de Michigan
Kaput – Quebrado
Limerick – Quintilla Cómica
Loot – Monedas
Majorette – Muchacha en la banda
Millionaire – Una persona con mucho dinero
New Year – Año Nuevo

Oh, God Bless You – Salud
Parade – Procesión
Pimple – Mancha en la cara
Prepare – Preparado
Rainbow – Arco Iris
Rump – Culo
Sausage – Salchicha
Sculptor – Escultor
Shout – Gritar
Sidewalk – Acera
Slurred – Palabras alastradas
Sneeze – Estornudar
Soar – Volar
Somebody – Alguien
Speaks – Habla
Spilled – Botó
Timbuktu – Un lugar muy lejos
Today – Hoy
Too much – Demasiado
Toot – Sonido
Trace – Un poquito
Twins – Gemelos
Words – Palabras

GLOSARIO (ESPAÑOL–INGLES)

Abeja – Bee
Abuela – Grandmother
Ahorita – Right now
Ajo – Garlic
Albondigas – Meatballs
Ay, Dios Mio – "Oh My God"
Bandera – Flag
Cabeza – Head
Cantar – To Sing
Chiquitín – Tiny
Chocó – Crashed
Cocina – Kitchen
Culparon – Blamed
Deporte – Sport
Descansar – To rest
Dolor – Pain
Encanta – Enchant
Enero – January
Escuchar – To listen
Frijoles – Beans
Gente – People
Gallo Pinto – Rice and Beans mixture

Gastronómica – Having to do with the stomach
Impenetrable – Unreachable
Ladrando – Barking
Lápiz – Pencil
Lástima – What a shame!
Llorando – Crying
Nunca – Never
Parece – It seems
Peligroso – Dangerous
Pelota – Ball
Perros – Dogs
Pluma – Pen
Poderoso – Powerful
Por Supuesto – Of Course!
Prefiero – Prefer
Risa – Laughter
Quiere – Wants
Quintilla Cómica – Limerick
Simpático – Friendly
Tico – A man from Costa Rica

Also by Mama Bear Gina/Jeanne Crowley

The Very Droopy Honey Bear

Thanks to the colleagues,
students, family, and friends
whose words found their way
into my funny bone
and the limericks.

Gracias a los colegas,
los alumnos, mi familia, y mis amigos,
cuyos palabras se encontraron
en mi "hueso divertido"
y en las quintillas cómicas.

Printed in the United States
By Bookmasters